Copyright © 2023 Emma Keen

This book is copyright. This book or any portion thereof may not be reproduced or used in any manner whatsoever without the express written permission of the publisher except for the use of brief quotations in a book review. All rights reserved.

ISBN: 978-0-646-89120-0

https://alanandpenny.wordpress.com/

Disclaimer

The information in this book has been prepared in good faith and for educational purposes only. Therefore, the information is general in nature and should not be relied upon as a sole source of information, nor as a replacement for therapy. You should seek your own independent professional advice concerning any specific issues.

The authors accept no responsibility for any errors, omissions or decisions relating to the information.

for you, little bear

AHHHHHHHHHHHHHHHHHHHHHHH

Alan is an **AMYGDALA**. He lives in your brain. When he is surprised, or scared he can

REALLY

REALLY

REALLY

FREAK OUT

It looks like he has lost his friend Penny and might need some help!

Penny the parachute helps Alan to slow down. But, when Alan's worries are **ENORMOUS**, Penny can't land safely, and Alan needs Penny to turn off the alarm in his head!!

"I've tried **everything** to slow down! I've tried staring at the TV until my eyes are sore, I've tried making my heart pump really fast! I've tried breathing really quickly! But **nothing** is working!"

Lucky you're here! You can help Alan find Penny so he can go to bed.

First, put your hand on this page and tell Alan what you feel.

Does it feel SOFT or HARD?

Can you feel any LUMPS?

Any SMOOTH spots?

Good job! Let's try something else! If you have a tummy, put your hand on it.

Not the sticky hand, though!

Got it? Right, Penny **LOVES** air! So, can you breathe in until your tummy is bigger than the biggest balloon? Got it?

I think it's working!
I can see Penny!

Have you got any muscles?
Can you squeeze your fists together **REALLY** tight?

TIGHTER!

TIGHTER!

Now, hold that suqeeze and count to ten in the funniest voice you can make!

1... 2... 3... 4... 5... 6... 7... 8... 9... 10...

Wow! Now, how slowly can you let them go?

One last thing: Alan left his worry box open,

so all of the worries have **escaped!**

All you need to do now is concentrate on putting all the worries in the box and close the lid!

Now that you know how to help, you can do it anytime you need to help slow Alan down and turn his alarm off so Penny can land!

Alan

Alan the amygdala (sounds like **uh-mig-duh-lu**) is really helpful when we are running from tigers, when there are big scary things to get away from, and when we need to move really fast. He can also help us get ready for tests because he motivates us to study; he does a great job of helping us be prepared.

But he is not helpful for eating chocolate, talking to teachers, packing your school bag, or sleeping. He lives in the back of your brain, and he doesn't do so great at thinking either.

To help Alan slow down, you can do any of the activities from this book! You can use the green hand to ground you by using your senses when you are out and about to find as many green things as you can, or by using a fidget or a toy and naming what you can feel.

You can use your breath by breathing in for a count of three and then out for a count of five at least ten times. Try to breathe deep into your belly when you do this.

You can use your muscles to squeeze your hands like you're trying to squeeze the juice from lemons. Count to ten while you do this in a funny voice! When you get to ten, let them go really, really slowly. You can repeat this as many times as you like.

Penny

Penny the parachute is really helpful to slow us down. She lives in the front of our brain and is involved with the thinking 'logically' parts of our brain. She is really helpful for relaxation, making decisions, and helping Alan go to sleep. Penny is not helpful for running from tigers, running competitions, or fighting with your little sister.

Penny is really good at helping Alan close his worry box! Everyone has one! To find yours, imagine a box that is your favourite colour made out of something SUPER strong. Whenever Alan yells out a worry, practice putting the worry in the box in your head and locking it away for safekeeping. You can even make a real worry box and write your worries down for the box to gobble up! Make sure to ask an adult for help with this one.

Penny also loves talking. Did you know that if you talk about your worries with people who love you, they can help you to challenge these worries or put them in the worry box with you? There are even adults who talk to people about their worries as a part of their job and professionally help them! They are called psychologists and are great to talk to if you need some extra help shutting the lid of your worry box.

Dear Parents and Guardians,

Do you remember the last time you had a feeling of panic? A sense of overwhelming dread or a worry that you just couldn't control? Now imagine that situation again, but with no knowledge that it will ever get better, no control over the outcome, and no memory of the resources you would usually use to help you manage.

That's what anxiety can be like for children. This is especially true for younger children who really don't have a lot of control over their emotions and rely on their parents for – well – survival! It can feel to them like it will never end, that things will never get better, and they can't change it. As adults, we are able to look at times in our lives and gather evidence to say that how we are feeling at this moment will not last for all of eternity, as there have been times when things have been better. Children don't have these same resources. Instead, it's our job to be those resources for them.

When it comes to anxiety, managing physiological arousal can be a powerful tool to help calm the nervous system and regulate a child's emotions. In this book, Alan represents the amygdala, which sits within the limbic system of our brain. He also represents the activation of the sympathetic nervous system. Without going into the details of neuroscience, these structures are linked to our fight, flight, and active freeze responses. When this system is activated, our brain and body are both geared towards survival; like running from a sabre tooth tiger kind of survival. It's not geared towards thinking logically or making decisions. And as you would know, you cannot run from a tiger and sleep at the same time. Penny, on the other hand, is representative of our prefrontal cortex (the very front of our brain that regulates our thoughts, actions, and emotions) and parasympathetic nervous system (our rest/homeostasis system). If we learn to activate her and open the parachute, we can let Alan have a rest, and we are generally more grounded, logical, and able to problem-solve, rather than just run around manically.

Finally, one of the most powerful tactics we can use with anxiety is to see it as being outside of ourselves. This can decrease the feelings of being overwhelmed because we stop trying to change who we and instead develop a different way to respond to an emotional experience. If we can increase resources, we can increase control and resilience. and So go forth, notice when Alan takes over, name it, then invite Penny back in by using a few strategies. She's much more reasonable.

ABOUT THE AUTHOR

Emma is a psychologist with a passion for increasing mental health literacy in children. She has worked in the mental health field with children and families for over fifteen years and understands the power of creating characters to help explore big feelings and increase strategies to help along the way.

After Emma became a mother, she was searching for a way to describe common concerns with her son to help him learn about his nervous system, the power of his emotions and skills to work through the hard ones.

Now, they create stories together about Alan and Penny and take the two on wonderful adventures that are shared with you!

www.ingramcontent.com/pod-product-compliance
Lightning Source LLC
Chambersburg PA
CBHW061808290426
44109CB00031B/2970